BLAST SKY

BY TOMMY TUCKER

Pounding My Head on the Steering Wheel of Life

Blast Sky

BLAST SKY

TOMMY TUCKER

Hand Cranked Books
Texas

BLAST SKY.

Copyright © 2025 by Tommy Tucker

All rights reserved. Printed in the United States of America. No part of this book may be used or reproduced in any manner whatsoever without written permission except in the case of brief quotations embodied in critical articles and reviews.

For information, contact the publisher at handcrankedbooks@gmail.com or
Hand Cranked Books LLC, PO Box 49, Fischer, TX 78623

www.handcrankedbooks.com

First U.S. Edition

Cover illustration by VanArk Collective.

ISBN 978-1-941717-03-5 (trade paper)

ISBN 978-1-941717-04-2 (electronic)

for Mum and Dad
Thank you for giving me this world

CONTENTS

CITIES OF PYRITE

I

West Texas Grit	7
Kingman, AZ	9
Drink / Before Air Bags	10
Killer Bees Please	12
In the Desert Southwest	15
Coronado	16

II

Dog Bark Breath	21
A Loose Penchant for Words	23
Wisdom	24
No Time, Time Enough	25
Sounds Not at All	26
Babel	27
Universal Mutterings	29
Stone Rollin	30

COLUMNS OF DUST

III

The Horror ...	35
Blood in the Coffee	37
The Crow of My Youth	39
Mouse / Mice / Louse	41
The Future's Too Late	42
Wording	43
Night Prayers	44
Bleed the Sky	45
The Size of Those Teeth	46
Cargo	47

IV

Cyclical / Alone with the Drowned	51
Noose	53
Hush	54
Threat of Dog	56
Reading Poetry Is Not Easy	57
You Can't Go Back	59
Dark Matter	62
Anonymous	63

BLAST SKY

CITIES OF PYRITE

I

West Texas Grit

Wind kicks up, gusts
up to 65 MPH,
cold front behind,
planes diverted, birds
struggle to gain
high-line perches, clouds
hustle across a skid
blue sky.
          The wind
carries dust and memories
from West Texas: standing,
trying not to bend,
but the wind
always winning
and always hot,
drying the skin,
scraping the land; a sudden
thunderstorm
grabbing the dirt and
throwing it back down,
the rainwater brown and
heavy in the palm.

Another memory: a door
torn from the hand,
crumpled against the side
of the house, the aluminum

bent in half, the screen
loose and racing across
scoured land that harbored
my cousin until seven
weeks ago when he fell
upon the red-brown earth,
its dust chewing his teeth
and insides. It always
gets in there. It always
finds you. Look how it's
found me.

Kingman, AZ

Face down drunk in a travel trailer
forgotten well beyond the edge of town. Outside,
the stars kick around on the desert floor,
startle the dogs who howl at coyotes.
And the coyotes howl at the moon
which stays well away up in the sky.
By proximity, the moon knows better
than the stars will ever know
that man grabs all that is beautiful,
bites out whole chunks and spits forth
musty paste we spend entire lives shaping
into the thing lying here on the bathroom floor,
barely breathing but counting just the same.

Drink / Before Air Bags

Sometimes you get lucky and the orange
juice tastes like orange juice and not
something not like orange juice.

Sometimes the tires grab hold the bit
of pavement poking through the ice
and the car stays on the road
instead of crashing through barbed
wire and hitting a small mesquite
tree with tremendous force and
killing your best friend behind the
wheel and the girl in the back seat
both of you barely knew. You stumble
out of the car. The moon escorts
you. Your breath puffs out like
steam. You feel hot. You feel
cold. Later you are told you were
in shock – no shit! – and you were
bleeding from two cuts to your
head. None of this will matter of
course – you will be counted
lucky but you will think otherwise
seeing over and over your friend
gnarled into windshield glass,
face, hands, upper chest stripped away.
All of this will come later. Right
now ... right now you walk

in the lighted white way of the
moon. You try to catch the
puffs of steam and put them
back in your mouth. You walk
and walk. You try to imagine
you are dreaming and none of
what you know just happened
did happen. You walk.

You stop.

You turn around, part of you coming
awake. Help. You must help. There
is hope. There are people with magical
medical skills. There are miracles.
You cannot see the twisted metal and
fiberglass from which you were
born. You see only mesquite trees
with their inch long needles waiting
for the moon to vanish so they can stab
over and over and drink you up.

Killer Bees Please

The killer bees
had worked
their way
north.
So he decided
to drive down and
greet them just south
of the border.

Really, he was
down there to
escape the crap-ass
town he was living
in (10,000 people,
that many churches,
17 factories making
paint and plastics).
He and his girl
took their two paychecks
and drove all night
through white Arizona,
crossed the line,
caught the water-
less coast,
followed it to
sleepy fishing

village San Felipe.

That first morning
they ate omelets
buried in slices
of avocados – green
all over the plate –
watched men
drive pickup trucks,
gasoline cradled
in milk jugs the driver
held out his
window, tubes
snaking under
the hood, feeding
the engine, running
their lives, the boys
in the pickup bed
grinning
at the gringos
staring in awe
at the simplicity
of it all, never
mind the god-
damned bees.

But they won't let go,
the bees clumped to
the only tree

down at the pier
where he and the girl sat
one afternoon,
drinking beers,
and people rushed
past, their rapid
Spanish just a buzz to him
but the girl said, *Bees.*
And he saw them
bunched on the skinny
lonely tree. He stood
and – *stupid drunk gringo
culo turista fool* –
went to the bees and
watched them crawl and
hum all over each other
as men abandoned chairs,
fled past. He looked over
his shoulder at the men
clumped at the far end
of the pier well past his girl
who sat with legs crossed. She
drank his beer, smiled, thought, too,
that he was a fool. Later, the bees
gassed and dead, he studied
the top of her head, her thick
wavy hair like killer bees
crawling all over themselves,
oblivious to gringos
going and coming.

In the Desert Southwest

Harbors in these parts consist
of truck stops – massive, dirty
beasts upon the land complete
with women and showers for rent,
diesel fuel in great and seemingly unlimited quantities,
and (usually) horrible chicken fried steak.

A kid bounces a bouncy ball
against a wall with no windows.
I step forward and catch the ball.
I look up. The kid looks up.
We see the storm
galloping toward us,
snorting and sparking
apocalyptic fire.

Coronado

I'm lost in the Mojave
and think I might be
drunk until the guy one
over says we've just had
an aftershock to some
earthquake 300 miles
and seven hours
away. See, see, he says
to me and jabs at the dust
falling through the weak light
hanging out in every bar.
Bullshit, I mumble.
I need to piss but decide it best
to save my beer from this madman,
so I drink.

CORONADO IS COMING!
The drunk bastard screams
and rolls along the edge of the bar
like a deranged Ahab.
HE'S RIDING A HORSE
SPIKED WITH DIAMONDS AND
DEAD CHEROKEE!
AND WALKING BEHIND HIM,
A THOUSAND VIRGINS,
GOD ALMIGHTY YES!

Choking on startled foam,
I push my beer away
and head through
glittering particles
for the exit. One can only take
so much wishful thinking,
so many earthquakes
and entourages of virgins.
Like any man
would allow such a thing –
especially Coronado,
whoever the fuck he really was.

Later, still lost, I
stop at the side of the
road and send my piss
arcing into the desert,
listen to the ground
crunch around the sudden
moisture. Though befuddled
in my direction, I still
admire the void of night
all around me.

I tuck, turn back
to the car, wobble,
and drop to one knee.
My bracing hand
feels the ripple
run beneath me,

move up, clang my teeth together.
Jesus, I think. And then, No,
as I see light bouncing toward me.
But whether off the
diamonds, the pure pussy,
or the glazed eyes
of a thousand Cherokees,

I never know.

II

Dog Bark Breath

I get up
to let him in.
Cold air follows,
strikes my chest,
catches my breath.

I step out into
the yard's darkness,
no harbor in sight.
Safe inside, the dog
watches my trek.
If I return not,
he will simply go to his
blanket, lie down,
snore through the
rest of the night.

In the morning,
search crews will
step into the backyard.
They will clutch at the ropes
tied to their waists.
They will know
before they are even done,
that they will not
find me. This knowledge
will dry the spit on their lips,

make their walkie-talkies
worthless. My yard quarantined,
the dog will pant at the back
door and not give a damn.

A Loose Penchant for Words

Cutting the shrubs
at the back perimeter
of the yard, I come
across a lizard, green,
slick, bigger than most.
It does not move, though
the shears hover
next to its head. Instead,
the slick green lizard
licks its lips.
It knows me:
a charlatan in this life,
a poser without the charm
of sports television,
incapacitated by the fear of
taking what I need. Inside
the house behind us,
a wife not a wife,
a hunger not a hunger.
I and the lizard stare
at each other, wait
for the other to make
the first move.

Wisdom

One night, years ago,
I wrote thirty-six poems.
The next morning
all the sheets were blank.
My pen was out of ink
and I was too drunk to notice.

In a burst of ingenuity,
I grabbed a pencil and
rubbed the lead flat
against all the paper.

Looked like alien speak,
rants and chicken screeches.
Yes, screeches.
My god I must've been drunk.
I was drunk that next morning
and still could not tell
a damned thing I wrote
from the atoms of non-ink
bent into the atoms of paper.

Despair tried to take hold,
but I flipped the sheets over,
started scribbling again.
Waste not want not,
some drunk bastard once said.

No Time, Time Enough

I keep losing my copy
of *The Old Man and the Sea*.
Just the other day, I wanted
to get my youngest to read it,
but it was not on the shelves
with the other Hemingway.
My fingers hesitated along the spine
of *In Our Time* and *Kilimanjaro*,
but for an eleven-year-old,
nothing contends with the singular man
out in his boat surrounded by the sea,
fighting the fish below him,
finding his soul one last time,
the lions on the beach,
the cosmos in the sky
sparkling in their eyes.

Sounds Not at All

Pause and Double Pause
Money stares me in the face
And this, this blank, open-faced –
      though lined –
Book was to be for my thoughts
My ideas.

But here I am sullying it with my
Idea of Wisdom,
My idea of Hope, thought clenched
Between my teeth, struggling
      to get out –
But I'm not letting it.

Breast of my breast, hope of my hope,
I want to ramble and eat up the night
And not think of money and the fact
      that I'm way behind.
   but even worse: not as far behind as some,
As many: friends, family, the guy next door
Who last week threatened to put a shotgun
In his mouth – till his ex-wife called and
Screamed at him and he realized
Sometimes money is the least of problems.
The next day he called and had his telephone
      disconnected.
And I said, "Good move." And he said,
      "Yeah, maybe."

Babel

My kids make
drawings
in my note
books. I work
around them, my words
crawling amidst
their squiggles,
Soldiers,
and what look like
hyenas.

I hope
they don't mind:
either the screwing
of their perfect lines
or the blending
of our tongues
and eyes.

Do you see
what I see?
Do you hear
what I hear?

Like son, like father.

I reach a
soldier's foot
and stop, afraid
to go further – except

to sign their work
for them.

Universal Mutterings

My wife and I talk
on the phone during her break –
she in her building,
I in mine.

We have the same conversation
over and over.

I'm tired of being tired, she says.
I know, I say.

She sighs.
I wait.

Up above us,
the clouds gather
like mountains.

Stone Rollin

I go to bed exhausted
– not in a good way –
frustrated that tomorrow
and tomorrow
and the next day
will all be the same,
god-dammit.

I try and try
to comfort myself
with the thought
that most of us
can't make
the world spin
anyway.

Flashes of light
as I close my eyes.

Flashes of light
will one day
wake us
to a new morning.

COLUMNS OF DUST

III

The Horror ...

From the clutter
that is my desk
at work, two
blank pages
stare up at me

questioning

beckoning

pissing me off,
tickling my thoughts,
the electrons and piss-ant
neutrons
bouncing around my skull.

Peace be with you, my friends.
I try to toss the bastard duo
in the recycling bin (full, over-
flowing) next to my desk –
how much paper WASTED
on vacant numbers, hollowed ideas?
how many ivory pages to
every thrust? – but
the two pages slide, cling
to the industrial standard
Formica desk. So, I
take up pen and crush ink

into the former tree,
try o' try to
make its death (and mine)
somewhat worthwhile.

Blood in the Coffee

They interrogate me.
What keeps you going?
What? Oh ... coffee.
Coffee ... special coffee?
What's "special coffee"
and where can I get some?

They laugh, their own joke
playing funny for them.
They've read my bio.
I thought it was a joke
when a man said
people went out windows
when on the drink.
Then I tried to throw
my best friend through one,
except there was suddenly a
wall where I swore the window
was a moment earlier –
which was a good thing
considering.
One way or the other
there was blood
and my friend ... well, we
haven't talked in two decades.

Still laughing, the Europeans
pack away the last microphone, but

they don't smile when they leave.

It gets real quiet.

It's no joke.

The Crow of My Youth

The crow chased me – age of five –
across the dusty small town city park.
I ran and ran but it still dug its claws
into the top of my head
for the briefest moment
(forever it seemed).
I screamed,
hollered my way home,
my last glimpse back revealed
betrayal: mother laughing,
forsaking protection of her first-born.
She came home,
still chuckling,
casually pulling my head
from beneath saturated pillow,
calling what I knew to be
puncture wounds "barely
scratches." Mad at her, I
cursed the mad bird.
Mom reminded me it was a pet.
So what, it still tried
to grab me and lift
me up into the sky.
I burst into fresh tears.
Oh, mother said and held me close.

Years later, physics wiser, I spun
a humorous re-telling at

the holiday dinner table,
but Mom corrected me:
it was a pet raven, not a crow.

Betrayed again.

Mouse / Mice / Louse

In the middle of an on-line meeting,
demonstration, whatever – and also trying
to document someone's poor performance –
I hit that wall, over-load on words,
and turn away, stare at the wall.
The gray carpet-looking crap nauseates me
so I dig through the trash and pick out
some used hot sauce packets, smear
the remnants on several blank sheets of paper,
rub my fingers around in circles and lines.
No doubt I'm going mad. No doubt
we all should be.

The phone rings. I ignore it.
Shouldn't be calling during a "live demonstration"
of a tool that will only improve our efficiency
if we were all mice and then only every
third Thursday.

Jesus I need to get out of here.
Jesus I can't:
food clothing house
food clothing house
brood fucking mouse

The meeting ends but I only notice
much later, feet up, seat and head
tilted way back, eyes closed. They can't
have all of me, not all of the time, no sir.

The Future's Too Late

Making notes for future poems
never works. Tried it so many
times it's ridiculous – more so that
I keep trying.
                    Like the other day,
I found notes saying "parent-
teacher night" and "afraid of spiders."
Even if I knew what the fuck
my earlier self meant,
gone is the *umphf* that
hit me between the eyes
in the first place. You don't
have that, you don't have a poem.
You got a fucking
grocery list.
                    I crumpled the notes,
tossed 'em, told myself, The next
time you *stop*, you pull over, you write that
motherfucker until it's done.
Don't look back and especially DON'T
LOOK FORWARD.
There won't be time enough,
I told myself.

Guess we'll see ...

Wording

I come up with stupid titles and fill
two pages with them. Stupid stupid
horrible stuff. In the sofa chair
next to me, two women fill out forms,
talk occasionally to each other in the
Spanish language. I catch
a word or two, here and there:
"cinco"
"mas"
"tienes"
"aqui"
then "Alzheimer's."

There it is, the first
decent word of the day –
wakes up the senses, tightens
the throat, tingles fear
square in the middle
of the mind, thank God.

Night Prayers

Dog's face swells up,
eyes close shut. Up all night
watching Benadryl not do much good,
then a trip to the vet ER.
Their meds knock the reaction down.
We go home, collapse in bed.

Later, I hear my wife say,
"Don't leave me. You're leaving me."
I'm so tired, I mumble back but unsure
if she heard or not. Plus, you got it wrong ...

Later still, I wake, catch myself
in the bathroom mirror. The house is
empty of everything
except the bed, me and the dog
sprawled on the rug-less hardwood
like someone dropped him there.
I watch him ...
I wait for him to breathe...
to prove
that after all we've been through,
we're somehow still alive.

Bleed the Sky

The wind stirs up everything,
makes the kids sick,
blows trees into power lines
and power lines into trees.
Grocers and gas attendants
lean on brooms,
unable to strip
$ without electricity.
It's all a big mess.

I look down at scattered drops of blood.
Check nose, lips, mouth,
gums, ears, neck – even unbutton
my shirt and check for
bullet holes.

I look up
and see a slight gash
from debris thrown by the wind.
The sky isn't crying,
it's bleeding.
And I'm the unlucky fool
catching just a bit of its heart.

The Size of Those Teeth

They'll find me out on the streets.
My boys embarrassed, my wife
scratching her head, mumbling a little
to herself, calculating the
cost of resuscitation vs. just
calling it in, cashing the bonds
and life insurance, chucking
all my old books. The future
sparkles and her mumbling
of figures and costs turns to
hallelujahs of freedom.

The kids step back from her.

That's how it starts, baby:
talking to yourself, eyes
wide, the vast treasure
of time and space ahead,

ready to eat you.

Cargo

Semi-truck leans
far to the right.
Dangerous. I look
down at the tires
but see no flats nor
low pressure among
the eighteen. So
the cargo inside
is heavy or misshapen
or has come loose.
I imagine a monster
or nuclear missile
rolling around
in there, next to me ...

The traffic hiccups.
We move.

IV

Cyclical / Alone with the Drowned

The crickets are everywhere
And so are the locusts – the cicadas.

Last year *nothing*.
No buzz of insects.
No fireflies carousing the twilight yard.
No mosquitos biting my wife
and forcing her inside,
leaving me on the patio
with my thoughts ... alone.

Last summer, the heat murdered
everything before it could grow,
pupate,
spread,
harvest blood.

So, my wife hung with me, and I settled
into a crappy plastic desk chair
creaking beneath my weight
and the pressing, burning sun.

A wet spring preceded this summer
and the cicadas yipped
and climbed from burrowed hotels
and the crickets bred like
black, scaly rabbits and rubbed

their legs together exponentially
like my wife used to when
we were both younger.

This summer, I pick up
the cracked and faded
deck chair and throw it
in the god-damned trash.

And then quickly,
the locusts – the cicadas –
vanish when a hail-filled thunderstorm
pummels leaves from trees
punches holes in green-striped sides.

The crickets drown

The skies part and the sun's
honest wrath
blasts the land,
fires spill from cigarettes and random sparks,
dance across carpets of grass.
And I sit in my backyard,
alone
again
and wait for it all
to burn.

Noose

Unable to orient myself,
cannot find the sheet
at the bottom of the bed.
Late at night is always
best for birthing poems,
especially with a full moon.
Such as tonight …

In the pale morning, circles
of ink stain the blanket.
My wife gone, I wail and thrash
against the passing of time,
the sheet tangled round the neck,
the words strangled.

Hush

I pause to take a sip
of water, look out at the eyes
(mostly) looking at me.
In a fit of stupidity and honesty,
I admit all I do is write
of my stunned fear, head
scratchings of how I came to:
1) live in the suburbs,
2) get fat,
3) lose my hair,
4) be a crappy dad,
5) take Prozac (or one of those soma drugs),
6) wait to die.

All I get are blank eyes and
shakes of the head "Not
me" ... "No way" ... "Know better" ...
"Never me."

I want to insist, You don't know that.
Those who say "No"
have already said "Yes."
Because I did the same thing.

I reach for the glass of water –
wish for stronger, how I wish –
and take a gulp. Keep
reading, I tell myself. No more

insane sage advice, no more
warnings not heeded – you
didn't either, you fat fuck.
Remember that.
I raise the sheets of paper.
They flutter, my hands
an earthquake. Another sign,
old man. Close thy eyes
and recite. Let the words roll
right on out
until there's no one left
in the room.

NOTE: For some reason, I want to dedicate this silliness to Kevin Ayers, Skip Spence, Ollie Halsall and Syd Barrett: probably bastards, but ain't we all – and at least they were akin to diamonds scattered upon the broken beaches of time.

Threat of Dog

The dog wants out again.
Went just ten minutes ago but he
pants with desire for night air
and scents and other canine calls
barked across the darkness –
time a non-factor, always *now*.
I, on the other hand, see
clock hands, tell the dog *no*.

Disappointed, he burps in my face,
goes to his bed, circles, sleeps.
I, on the other hand, float
just above my bed, wait
for hemlock, genocide and
acid rain to make their comebacks.

My heart races ahead.

Reading Poetry Is Not Easy

I buy books of poems
in thrift store bargain bins,
dig 'em outta trash heaps,
scrape away fire-sale ashes.

I leave these tomes
all over the house
but mainly near the toilets.
Allows getting in a bite,
even during a piss.

But it's not easy getting
through a whole book of
poems, cause if they're good
you gotta take 'em slow.

And if they're bad, well,
then I gotta sneak back
into dumpsters, return
the charity, or re-start the fire
that went after them
in the first place.

The flames keep me warm
in the winter,
roast marshmallows with the kids
in the summer.
The words turn to smoke,

go back out there free,
try again to get closer
to the bone
to the heart
to the heat
of your soul.

You Can't Go Back

I find
some old poems
in the garage.

I sit down, peel
apart
the moldy pages,
ink running back
some twenty
years.

I copy them
onto fresh
pages, start
sliding
a word
or two around,
taking
some out,
dropping a
new one in
here ...
there ...

Then I
stop.

Who the fuck
am I
to think I
know
well enough
the person who
wrote these
poems?
Get yer aged
paws offa 'em.

Right.

I scoop up
the crass edits,
and throw
them into the
fireplace, strike
one of those
long matches
and burn the lot
of them.

My wife – bless
her heart
– comes home
from work, smells
the smoke, sees
the black
brittle
paper-thin ash

crumpled
on the grate
and says, You
made a fire
in July?

Everywhere a critic.

Dark Matter

Cosmos above,
reaching out.
I think of Wallace
and his ice cream,
Percy watching
a movie.

Think of my boys
playing vid games,
the light outside
fading. I think
of my death
closer and closer
every day. How
will I greet it?
What will I think
in those final
moments before
the ultimate
darkness:
my boys?
a favorite
movie scene?
mint chocolate chip
ice cream?

Anonymous

I try to stay awake,
get the last few words
on-board the last ship
leaving the port of night.

An owl calls to me.
I shiver. Poem and
words forgotten,
I stand next to the window
and wait for the owl
to speak again. Instead, he
opens wide his beak
and swallows me,
my scant words,
the dying night.

VanArk Collective-CIA Files

TOMMY TUCKER grew up in the 70s and 80s digesting heavy doses of Cold War rhetoric and flashpoint conflict. Each day the whole world teetered on news proclaiming nuclear war and movies dishing out full-blown apocalypse. It was enough to drive one into a bunker to write goodbye notes.

Blast Sky includes poems written during the years 2011 to 2014. Signed copies might be stashed in fallout shelters of the nearest buildings. If such things exist anymore ...

www.ingramcontent.com/pod-product-compliance
Lightning Source LLC
Chambersburg PA
CBHW030532080526
44586CB00011B/411